MAKERSPACE SURVI

MAKE IT
OUT ALIVE
ON A
DESERT
ISLAND

Claudia Martin

PowerKiDS press.
New York

Published in 2018 by The Rosen Publishing Group
29 East 21st Street, New York, NY 10010

Produced for Rosen by Calcium
Editors: Sarah Eason and Jennifer Sanderson
Designer: Emma DeBanks
Picture Research: Rachel Blount
Illustrator: Venetia Dean

Picture credits: Cover: Shutterstock: Iakov Kalinin (bg), Peter Waters (br). Inside: Shutterstock: Poprotskiy
Alexey 42–43, Shevelev Alexey 18, Valentin Ayupov 26, Thomas Barrat 13, Diana Chiriac 38, Erni 20,
Foodonwhite 25br, GavranBoris 22, Ivancreative 5c, Alexandr Kazharski 14, Michal Knitl 36, Anatoly Kovtun
21, Kanyapak Lim 28, Lisaveya 23, R McIntyre 7, Montego 15, Nudiblue 17, Orla 44, Pablofdezr 6, Photo
Image 40, Pikselstock 41, Andrey Polivanov 35, Valentina Razumova 24b, 47, JeremyRichards 10, Samot 30,
Serg64 5tr, Eugene Sergeev 24–25, Shebeko 31, Sheykhan 5b, Joshua Stills 16, Robert Szymanski 8–9, 9cr,
Teekevphotography 32, THPStock 4br, Totajla 4b, Ventura 37, Warmer 12, Wk1003mike 34; Wikimedia
Commons: 11, CDC/ Frank Collins 27, Marine Biological Association of the United Kingdom 43t.

Cataloging-in-Publication Data
Names: Martin, Claudia.
Title: Make it out alive on a desert island / Claudia Martin.
Description: New York : PowerKids Press, 2018. | Series: Makerspace survival | Includes index.
Identifiers: ISBN 9781499434774 (pbk.) | ISBN 9781499434712 (library bound) | ISBN 9781499434590 (6
pack)
Subjects: LCSH: Desert survival--Juvenile literature. | Shipwreck survival--Juvenile literature.
Classification: LCC GV200.5 M35 2018 | DDC 613.6'9--dc23

Manufactured in China.

CPSIA Compliance Information: Batch BS17PK: For Further Information contact Rosen Publishing, New
York, New York at 1-800-237-9932

Please note that the publisher **does not**
suggest readers carry out any practical
application of the Can You Make It?
activities and any other survival
activities in this book.

A note about measurements:
Measurements are given in U.S.
form with metric in parentheses.
The metric conversion is rounded
to make it easier to measure.

CONTENTS

CHAPTER 1
SURVIVE
A DESERT ISLAND

You are about to be abandoned on a desert island. A desert island is an **uninhabited** island. By yourself, you must find a way to survive until you are rescued. To make your mission even more difficult, you cannot take any food, drink, a tent, or cooking equipment.

Will You Make It Out Alive?

We are leaving you with two tools: an ax and a mirror. You can dress in your choice of clothing and footwear. Apart from these essentials, you must provide yourself with food, water, and shelter by making your own equipment. You are allowed to use any local materials you find on the island, as well as any recyclable man-made objects that wash ashore. We are also providing you with a backpack in which you will find some interesting materials and tools.

*Among the nastiest biting insects found on desert islands are the giant centipedes, which can kill animals as large as bats and frogs with their **venomous** bite.*

What resources will you find on your island?

What Is in Your Backpack?

The following materials and tools are in your backpack. When you come across a "Can You Make It?" activity in this book, you must choose from these items to construct it. Each material can be used only once. Study the list carefully before you set off. You can find the correct solutions for all the activities on page 45.

Can You Make It?

Materials
- 2 broom handles
- 20 metal bottle caps
- Coil of rope
- Thread
- Duct tape
- Large plastic bottle
- Nylon netting, 13 x 9 feet (4 x 3 m)
- Table tennis racket
- Sewing needle
- Strong cord, 7 feet (2 m) long

Table tennis racket

Sewing needle

Pair of scissors

Tools
- Craft knife
- Pair of scissors

Survival Tip
Use the Internet to look up all the items in your backpack before you begin your journey. Make sure you understand what they are and how you might be able to use them.

WORLD OF ISLANDS

Before you become a **castaway**, take a few minutes to learn about the environment you will be facing. There are more than one million islands in the world, some just a few feet across.

What Is an Island?

An island is an area of land surrounded by a lake, river, or ocean. Larger islands, which are often inhabited, are usually continental islands. These are part of the same block of land as a nearby **continent**, but the land surrounding them has **submerged**. Remote, uninhabited islands are likely to be oceanic islands, which have formed far from any continent. Many of them, called volcanic islands, were made by underwater volcanoes. When the volcano erupted, it spewed molten rock called lava. The lava hardened and, over time, grew above the water. The islands of Hawaii are volcanic islands.

HAWAII (USA)

NORTHERN MARIANA ISLANDS

MICRONESIA

FEDERATED STATES OF MICRONESIA

PALAU

MARSHALL ISLANDS

ASIA

NAURU   KIRIBATI

PAPUA NEW GUINEA

SALOMON ISLANDS

TUVALU

POLYNESIA

MELANESIA

SAMOA

COOK ISLANDS (NZ)

VANUATU   FIJI   TONGA

FRENCH POLYNESIA

NEW CALEDONIA (FR)

NIUE (NZ)

PITCAIRN ISLANDS (UK)

AUSTRALIA

AUSTRALASIA

NEW ZEALAND

CHATHAM ISLANDS (NZ)

The Pacific Ocean has several large continental islands, including New Zealand. There are also thousands of small oceanic islands, such as the volcanic islands of Hawaii.

In **tropical** seas, an atoll is an island made from a **coral reef** that grew around a volcanic island over millions of years. The volcano has sunk beneath the waves, but the reef, hardened into rock and worn into sand, remains.

Challenging Places

Oceanic islands are often rainy and windy. This is because the wind blows unchecked across the vast ocean, picking up moisture from seawater. Islands formed from coral are small and not high above **sea level**. They are at risk from flooding during tropical storms. They may not have a source of freshwater. A larger island may have streams, and **groundwater** from rain soaking into the soil.

Remote islands often have a small or unusual group of plants and animals. When an island forms, it is barren. Over thousands of years, plant seeds are carried there by the wind and waves, and on the feathers of birds and the fur of seals. Swimming and flying animals will arrive soonest, but large land-dwelling animals will arrive only if they are brought by humans.

These atolls are in the Maldives, an island country in the Indian Ocean. The Maldives is the world's lowest country, reaching only 94 inches (2 m) above sea level.

ISLAND PEOPLES

Life is difficult on remote islands, but some peoples, such as the I-Kiribati of Kiribati in the Pacific Ocean, make them their home. We can learn a few tips from the I-Kiribati about using maker skills to harness all the resources available.

Hostile Home

Kiribati is made up of 33 coral islands, spread over an area as large as the continental United States. Although there are only 313 square miles (811 sq km) of land, the coastline is 710 miles (1,143 km) long. These islands are just a few thousand years old, so only 70 to 80 plant **species** grow wild. The soil is thin and salty, and it soaks up little of the rain that falls. Only the **hardiest** crops can be planted. Humans have brought the only land **mammals**, such as pigs, to the islands. The I-Kiribati must turn to the sea for most of their food.

*Balanced by its float, the **hull** of a Kiribati canoe can be narrower than on an ordinary canoe. This sleek shape lets it cut through the water faster.*

Building Boats

Among the few wild plants in Kiribati are coconut and pandanus palms, as well as breadfruit trees. The I-Kiribati use the fruits of these trees for food and drink, and the wood and **fiber** for construction. I-Kiribati fishermen build **outrigger canoes** from planks of coconut palm and other **native** trees. Outriggers have a frame attached to a float on one side, which gives greater stability. In Kiribati, the float is made from the breadfruit tree. Everything is lashed together with rope made by braiding the hairy fibers on coconut husks. Traditionally, sails are woven from pandanus leaves.

Building Homes

Homes on Kiribati are built from the trunks of coconut trees, tied with coconut rope. Roofs are thatched with pandanus leaves. Since the islands straddle the equator, the temperature averages 82° F (28° C) throughout the year. Homes have open sides to allow the breeze to blow through.

Homes in Kiribati are built on stilts to protect them from the waves.

FIERCE FACT!
The I-Kiribati have bought land on a larger island. They will move to this land if their islands are submerged by rising sea levels caused by global warming.

ISLAND SURVIVOR

The most famous fictional castaway is Robinson Crusoe, whose adventures were written by Daniel Defoe in 1719. The real-life castaway Alexander Selkirk, who survived for four years on a remote island, is thought to have inspired Defoe's book.

An Argument

Selkirk was a Scottish sailor who, in 1704, was abandoned by his captain on an uninhabited island in the South Pacific Ocean. The two had argued when Selkirk complained that their ship was not seaworthy. He was correct. A month after Selkirk was **marooned**, the ship sank. Luckily, Selkirk was allowed to take some possessions onto the island, including his **musket**.

Selkirk's island, Isla Alejandro Selkirk, lies about 530 miles (853 km) west of the coast of Chile.

Making Himself Survive

At first, Selkirk waited alone on the shore, hoping for rescue and catching spiny lobsters to eat. He knew that escape on a raft was impossible, as the nearest inhabited land was hundreds of miles away. Finally, Selkirk realized he must move inland to find freshwater and food.

Selkirk made a knife from the metal hoops around the wooden barrels that washed up on the beach. Earlier sailors had released goats on the island. Selkirk used his musket to kill them and his knife to cut up their carcasses. When his clothes wore out, Selkirk made new ones from goatskin, stitched with a nail and grasses. He collected wild cabbage, turnips, and plums. He built himself two shelters from the trunks of pepper trees, sleeping in one and cooking in the other. Eventually, Selkirk saw an English ship and ran along the beach waving a burning branch to attract attention. When he returned home, Selkirk was a celebrity.

FIERCE FACT!
Sailors often released pairs of pigs, goats, or rabbits on uninhabited islands, so that there would be food to hunt when they returned.

Selkirk read his Bible in the shelter of his pepper tree hut.

CHAPTER 2
USE THE SEA

You find yourself on the beach of a remote, uninhabited island. Your challenge has begun! First of all, turn to the sea to make use of all the resources that it offers a thirsty, hungry castaway.

First Things First

Your most urgent need is to find drinking water and food. On a coral atoll, the sea may be the only source of both. Examine your island. If it is flat and there are no trees and little vegetation, it is unlikely you will find freshwater or many resources on land. Trees are a sign of groundwater, since they must draw up large quantities of water through their roots to survive. If there is vegetation, there will also be insect life and perhaps larger animals.

Take a walk along the beach. Collect driftwood and any man-made objects that have washed ashore, as they may be useful later. Are there rocks near the water's edge where mussels or barnacles have attached themselves? Other shellfish, such as cockles and clams, may be hiding under the damp sand. If shellfish is hard to dislodge from its rock or hard to open, it is usually safe to eat, once it is thoroughly cooked. Search rock pools for crabs and shrimp. Small creatures often cling to the seaweed that drifts ashore. All these finds can form your first meal.

Barnacles are shelled sea creatures that attach themselves to hard surfaces. All shellfish must be cooked before eating.

Use for a Mirror

To cook your food and to make drinking water out of seawater, you must light a fire. You do not have any matches, but you do have a mirror. Use it to reflect the sun's rays onto a pile of tinder. Tinder is any dry material that will catch on fire easily, such as bark shavings, straw, or small scraps of cloth. Even in bright sunlight, you will need to hold the mirror in place for several minutes before the tinder smokes and flames.

When your tinder is burning, feed your fire with fuel, such as driftwood, branches, or as a last resort, garbage washed up on the beach.

TOO SALTY

If there is no source of freshwater on your island, you will have to find a method of turning seawater into drinking water. Never drink seawater without first **distilling** it to get rid of the salt.

You Need Freshwater

Your body needs freshwater to survive. If you drink saltwater, your kidneys will try to get rid of the salt by washing it out in your urine. To do this cleaning job, your kidneys will take water from the rest of your body. If you do not drink freshwater to replace that lost water, you will become **dehydrated**. Luckily, now that you have your fire going, it is a straightforward job to make freshwater.

When water boils, water vapor **evaporates** from the surface. It is often called steam.

A Use for Soda Cans

Collect two empty soda cans that have washed up on the beach, along with some plastic tubing. Food cans or plastic bottles would also work. To make a **still**, half-fill the first can with seawater, and press one end of the tubing inside its lid. Wrap aluminum foil or a similar material around the tubing, sealing the top. Place the other end of the tubing in the other soda can. Hang the first can over the fire.

When the seawater in the first can boils, water evaporates from the surface. This means it turns from a liquid into a gas called water vapor. As it does so, the water leaves behind its salt. The water vapor travels along the tube. By the time it reaches the other can, it will be cooling down. As it cools, the water vapor **condenses**. This means it turns back into a liquid. It will take about three hours to collect a cup of pure water. Make some modifications to your still, so that it is as effective as possible.

Two soda cans can be turned into a still for distilling water.

FIERCE FACT!
Around 14 billion pounds (6 billion kg) of garbage gets dumped in the ocean every year, including millions of aluminum cans.

SHALLOW WATERS

The shallow water around your island is a perfect place to find fish to cook over your fire. You do not have a fishing net or rod, but there are plenty of other ways you can land a catch.

Safety First

Before you wade into the water, you need to protect your feet and legs. Hazards in the shallows include stinging jellyfish, sharp coral, and prickly, spined fish. An injury could become a life-threatening infection. If you brought rubber boots, they will be ideal. If not, examine the materials washed up on the beach for anything that could be useful. An old rubber tire could be tied around your feet and legs.

Even shallow water can be dangerous. Here, a rip current (center left) is rushing out to sea.

Keep in mind that there may be dangerous **currents** just offshore, which could pull you farther out. These are called rip currents. They often occur when breaking waves are large and powerful. All the water flows along the shoreline until it finds an exit route back out to sea, pulling swimmers with it. If caught in a rip current, do not try to swim against the flow. Instead, swim sideways, parallel to the beach, to move out of the current. Also keep an eye out for rising **tides**. Remember that even a knee-high wave could knock you off your feet.

Hiding Fish

Fish like to hide in shady areas, underneath overhanging rocks and branches or among seaweed. Fish are plentiful around coral reefs, but bear in mind that many reef fish are poisonous. Poisonous fish may look different from ordinary fish, with beaklike mouths, spines, rough scales, or bony plates. When you have located a good spot to fish, you will need a scoop, made from your clothing, a plastic bag, or any large container. Hold your scoop still in the water until a fish swims inside.

Yellow goatfish are common in coral reefs. Although they are often eaten, some goatfish cause a nasty stomach upset.

TRAP FISH

Building a fish trap is a labor-saving way of catching fish. A well-constructed trap will supply you with food every day. If you catch more fish than you need to survive, you can release them unharmed.

Trap Time

The idea of a trap is that fish can swim inside but are unable to swim out again. The simplest and oldest traps are V-shaped stone walls built in the intertidal zone. The intertidal zone is the area between the beach's high-tide mark (which can be spotted by the line of wet sand and driftwood) and the low-tide mark (the farthest the sea goes out). The open end of the V faces up the beach. When the tide is high, fish swim into the trap. When the sea withdraws, fish cannot exit the stone walls. Smaller traps that are easily moved can be placed in the shallows, wedged into a coral reef, or in a stream.

I-Kiribati fishermen built this heart-shaped trap. Water and fish flow into the heart at high tide. As the tide goes out, water drains from the trap through the opening, but most fish cannot find the exit.

Make a Fish Trap

From the supplies in your backpack and local materials, you will need to make:

→ A portable trap that small fish can enter but not easily exit
→ A method of weighing down the trap.

Can You Make It?

Step 1
Think about which item from your backpack could be turned into a small fish trap.

Step 2
Using a tool from your backpack, consider how you can shape this item to form a narrow entrance and a holding chamber.

Step 3
Put some old food or a dead insect in the trap as bait.

Step 4
Consider which local materials you could use to hold your trap on the seabed.

Holding chamber

Entrance

Bait

CHAPTER 3
USE THE LAND

The larger your island, the greater the chance that you will find usable resources inland. Leave the beach and explore, keeping an eye out for anything that you could put to use.

Animal Aware

You do not yet know what animals have **colonized** this island. Some island animals could be a threat to you. For example, on Komodo and nearby islands in Southeast Asia, you will find giant lizards known as Komodo dragons. They prey on animals as big as deer and could give you a life-threatening bite. Alternatively, there may be a colony of pigs or goats, whose ancestors were released by sailors centuries ago. Rats might overrun the island. Rats are common on board ships, so sailors can accidentally release them. Rats can destroy the balance of nature on an island, killing other species.

Look for animal tracks to help you figure out the dangers and resources on your island. Animals in the cat or dog family will leave paw prints with separate toe marks. Sometimes, claws marks will be visible if you are tracking a meat eater. Deer, sheep, goats, and pigs leave hoof prints. A slithering trail in soft sand may belong to a snake. Large lizards, such as Komodo dragons, may leave a track as they drag their tail behind them.

Komodo dragons are the largest species of lizard. They grow up to 10 feet (3 m) long.

The black rat is native to Asia, but today it is found all around the world.

A Life-or-Death Situation

Once you have figured out which animals would be good to eat, consider how you could trap them. For any trap, you need food as bait. You also need a means of closing a trap when the animal is inside. Consider how you could make a trap from local materials, such as branches and grasses, or using a hole in the ground. You should never trap animals unless you are in a genuine survival situation.

FIERCE FACT!
The Romans may have accidentally carried black rats to the Italian island of Montecristo. Over the centuries, the rat colony grew to 12 million.

DRIP, DRIP

Rain is likely to be your key source of drinking water during your stay on the island. Rain can be collected as it falls, particularly during a tropical storm, or in the form of groundwater.

Water Tanks

Use any clean containers to catch rainwater. Even your shoes can be used if you cannot find anything else. A washed-up wooden crate lined with plastic, such as a garbage bag or waterproof poncho, could make a permanent water tank. Alternatively, dig a hole, and line it with stones or plastic. The simplest rainwater collection system is to tilt large leaves, so that the water drips off them into a container.

To find running water, such as streams and springs, walk inland or uphill. A spring is where water flows directly from an **aquifer** to the ground's surface. An aquifer is a layer of below-ground rock that holds a large amount of water. The water is rain that has soaked into the ground. Streams may start at a spring, or they may flow from lakes or snow-capped mountains.

Use a clean container to collect rainwater during a storm.

Digging Wells

For thousands of years, people have been digging wells to reach the water in aquifers. Alone and with few tools, you are likely to find well-digging too exhausting and dangerous. Depending on the level of the groundwater, a well may need to be just 10 feet (3 m) deep or as much as 60 feet (18 m). If you were to dig deep enough, the hole would fill with water. You would need to line the hole with stones to keep the water from getting muddy. Wells are not a possibility on an atoll that rises only a few feet above sea level, since the soil will be too thin to hold water.

FIERCE FACT!
Water is probably not clean unless it has fallen straight out of the sky. Boil it for 2–3 minutes before you drink it.

How deep will you need to dig before you hit water?

PARADISE
PALMS

When you imagine a desert island, you probably think of a palm-fringed beach. Palm trees are often found on oceanic islands in tropical and warm regions. Knowing how to recognize and use palm trees is an important skill.

Many Uses

Although some of the 3,000 plants in the palm family are shrubs or vines, most palms are trees. They can be recognized by their unbranched trunk and their fan or feather-shaped leaves. Many palms are hardy, with seeds that are carried easily across the ocean to remote islands. For example, coconuts can float for hundreds of miles on ocean currents. When they reach land, they germinate, or start to grow, into a new tree.

Although all palms produce fruit, not all are safe to eat. Tasty fruits include dates and purple berrylike acai fruit. In many palm species, the trunk is covered with strong fibers that can be braided into rope. The leaves of most palms are large and strong enough to be used for roofs or sails.

Chocolatey-tasting acai fruits can be eaten or squeezed for their juice.

Dates hang in clusters from date palms. Date leaves are used to weave mats, baskets, and roofs.

Delicious Coconut

Keep an eye out for coconut palms. The hard-shelled fruits of this tree are an excellent source of water. Smaller coconuts, higher up the tree, contain more water and less oil. Larger coconuts may not be as good at quenching your thirst, but the oil is **nutritious**. To open a coconut, find the "seam" that runs around its center. Tap the seam against a hard surface, rotate, then tap again, continuing until the fruit splits open. Do this over a bowl to catch the milk. Do not forget to eat the white coconut flesh. The empty shell can be turned into a container for catching rainwater.

Coconut flesh is eaten raw or used in a sauce or dessert.

CHAPTER 4
BUILD SHELTER

Before you settle down for the night, you must build a shelter to protect yourself from rain and storms. The temperature will drop when the sun goes down, so you may be grateful for the warmth.

Stormy Seas

The climate of your island will depend on whether it is in cold or tropical waters. However, throughout the year, the surrounding sea will moderate your island's temperature. The water will cool it in the hot summer and warm it in the winter. Wherever your island is, rain will fall more frequently than it does over the interiors of continents, because the ocean is a constant source of moisture.

If you are in the tropics, you will be at risk from hurricanes, which are huge spiraling storms that form over warm waters. They happen when the hot, damp air rises quickly, making walls of cloud and rain. The storm starts to spin around a calm center called the eye. Hurricanes bring not only rain and powerful winds but also high waves and flooding.

A storm is gathering on the horizon. Can you build a shelter before it hits land?

Pick Your Spot

The beach is the lowest part of your island, and so it is the most at risk from flooding. Walk inland and uphill to find a good place to camp. This will also give you a break from the painful bites of sand flies, which are a pest on many beaches around the world. Avoid camping on swampy ground or near a still pool of water, since these will also harbor biting insects.

Before deciding on a spot, examine the landscape, and avoid any dry stream beds or ravines that could turn into rivers in the event of heavy rain. Also beware camping directly under coconut palms, which could drop their heavy fruit while you sleep.

FIERCE FACT!
Hurricanes can be up to 1,200 miles (1,900 km) wide and bring winds as fast as 215 miles per hour (346 km/h), flattening trees and buildings.

Female sand flies suck blood in order to make eggs. Blood is filling the see-through abdomen of this Phlebotomus papatasi *sand fly.*

RAISED BED

Building yourself a raised bed will keep you off the damp ground and out of the reach of crawling insects, spiders, and snakes. During the day, you can use your bed as a bench for resting and eating.

A Strong Structure

It is challenging, but not impossible, to build yourself a raised bed purely from local materials. You will need two strong, straight branches to act as the frame. Make yourself some rope from vines or by braiding fibers ripped from the trunk of a palm tree. For cross supports running between the two branches, gather flexible but robust branches or stems, such as bamboo. These branches need to bend a little under your weight, or they will be too uncomfortable to sleep on. To add further comfort, cover your structure with leaves or hay, having shaken it thoroughly first to get rid of bugs. Wedge your bed between the branches of two trees, or construct stone posts on which to rest it.

If you are marooned for a long time, you could use your ax to construct a seating area from a single tree.

Make a Raised Bed

From the supplies in your backpack and local materials, you will need to make:

→ A strong frame for either side of your bed

→ A flexible but unbreakable network of cross supports.

Can You Make It?

Step 1

Think about which items from your backpack could be used as a frame.

Step 2

Which item could you use to create a crisscrossed net between the two sides of your frame? It must stick firmly to the frame and take your weight. Make sure your bed is wide enough to sleep on.

Step 3

With the same item used to create the crisscross net, add extra cross supports at the head end.

Step 4

Consider which local materials could build two platforms to support your bed.

Cross supports

Frame

Crisscrossed net

FINDERS KEEPERS

To build a shelter, find local materials that are suitable to use as a framework, as rope, and as roof thatching. Also hunt for natural features of the landscape that can serve as a basis for your structure.

Cave Comforts

Caves were shelters for some early people. Do not choose a beach cave for your sleeping place, since it is likely to be at risk from rising tides and waves. Avoid caves that are damp inside, as they will be home to insects and reptiles. Never crawl into tight spaces or journey far inside the rock. Check that the rock is not in danger of collapsing. If you light a fire, a cave will make a cozy home in bad weather, as the dry rock will become warm to the touch. Close off the entrance with a wall of sharpened sticks.

Build yourself a sunshade on the beach so that you can scan the horizon for rescue ships.

A-Frame Shelter

The A-frame is one of the simplest shelters to construct. First, use your ax to cut three strong branches to form your A-frame. You need a ridgepole, which will run across the top of the shelter, and two other branches for arms (in a downward-pointing V), which will form the entrance. The back of the ridgepole can rest on the ground or be propped in a tree if you want a taller shelter.

Now add ribs to your A-frame, spacing them evenly along your ridgepole. Bamboo stems are ideal. At the midpoint of each stem, cut away one side of its hollow structure. This will allow you to bend them into an upside-down V. Finally, thatch your roof with palm fronds or similar leaves. Palm fronds can be split in two, then ripped at either end to form a flexible rope to tie them with.

This A-frame uses eight branches as ribs to support the ridgepole.

PROTECT YOURSELF

You will find biting insects a problem wherever your island is situated, but if you are in the tropics, you will be particularly at risk from the diseases spread by mosquitoes. Make a mosquito net to protect yourself.

Mosquito Net

In infected regions, a mosquito's bite can carry diseases, such as **malaria** and **Zika virus**, from person to person. Even if the mosquitoes on your island do not carry disease, their bites are itchy and could become infected if you scratch them. Mosquitoes most often bite after the sun has gone down. For this reason, you are at risk when you are sleeping. Mosquito nets have a simple concept: a lightweight mesh with holes too small for an insect to pass through. The net needs to be hung from a rafter or propped up. It may need to be weighted around the bottom to keep it from blowing up.

If your shelter is sturdy enough, you could hang a hammock and mosquito net from the rafters.

Make a Mosquito Net

From the supplies in your backpack and local materials, you will need to make:

→ A mosquito net large enough to cover your raised bed
→ Small weights around the edges to hold it down
→ A means of suspending the net over your bed.

Can You Make It?

Step 1
Consider which item from your backpack could be used as a mosquito net. Think about its dimensions and how it will best cover your bed.

Step 2
Which items in your backpack could be used as small weights? Which items could you use to attach these weights?

Step 3
Which local materials could be used as posts at either end of your bed?

Step 4
Think about which item in your backpack could be tied between your posts so that the net can be draped over it.

Posts

Net

Weights

CHAPTER 5
SAIL AWAY

A crucial decision is whether to stay on your island and wait for rescue, or build a boat and sail away to find inhabited land. On your island, you have resources and the safety of solid ground, but will rescue ever arrive?

Where Is Your Life Jacket?

An important factor in your decision must be the fact that you do not have a life jacket. A float could be fashioned out of your pants, blown up with air and tied at the legs and waist. A float could also be carved from cork, which is the naturally **buoyant** bark of cork oaks. Kapok, which is the fluff that surrounds the seeds of the kapok tree, is also buoyant, but it should be covered in waterproof material. To be buoyant, a material must be less **dense** than the liquid it is in. This is often because it has pockets of empty space, or air, inside. However, remember that no homemade life jacket will be up to the standard of a modern life jacket that is made from waterproof nylon and filled with foam or air.

Kapok trees are found in tropical regions. What other buoyant materials might be on your island?

Watch the Waves

The weather is also an important consideration. In the tropics, there is often a rainy season, when torrential rain and tall waves would make traveling in a small boat too risky. In colder regions, winter storms could cause fast winds and waves as high as 50 feet (15 m).

Do you think the wind or ocean currents will carry you in the direction of inhabited land? Run a test by building a small raft with a bright flag attached to it. Push it out from the beach, and watch where it goes. Does it float in the direction of ships passing on the horizon, or is it instantly destroyed in the waves breaking on the rocky cliffs of your island?

FIERCE FACT!

Scientists have developed new materials called aerogels, which combine a superlight gel with gas. They are among the world's most buoyant solids.

Always note the weather conditions. Would you set out to sea in waves like this?

CANOE CARVING

Canoes are narrow boats, pointed at both ends and with an open top. They can be propelled by paddles or sometimes by a sail. To carve your own canoe, follow the example of the I-Kiribati and other island peoples.

Choosing Materials

Humans have been building canoes for thousands of years. About 3,000 years ago, people traveling by canoe colonized the islands of Polynesia, in the Pacific Ocean. Over several centuries, they had paddled eastward from Southeast Asia, about 3,000 miles (4,800 km) away.

This maker in Papua New Guinea is hollowing out a tree trunk for her canoe.

Early canoes were made of a hollowed-out tree trunk, called a dugout canoe, or of planks and bark attached to a wooden frame. In regions where wood was not available, people used reeds waterproofed with tar. The I-Kiribati make canoes using planks cut from strong, but light, local woods, held together with carefully carved joints and coconut fiber.

Deciding on a Design

The hull of a canoe is the main body of the boat. A canoe's narrow, pointed hull gives it a **streamlined** shape. The length and width of the hull will depend on the wood you can find, and how much room you need for yourself and your supplies. If you give your hull high sides, it will be harder for waves to wash on board. However, your canoe will be heavier and could be more easily rolled by crosswinds. Do not make your sides so high that you cannot paddle. If you carve your hull with a V-shaped bottom, it will move quickly through the water and be difficult to capsize. On the other hand, a flat-bottomed canoe will have more storage space and be easier to turn.

FIERCE FACT!
The word *canoe* comes from the Carib word for a dugout: *kenu*. The Caribs were early inhabitants of the Caribbean's Lesser Antilles islands.

Modern canoes, which are often used for sports, are made from lightweight man-made materials, such as fiberglass or plastic.

RAFT BUILDING

Constructing a raft is simpler and faster than carving a canoe. However, a raft is harder to maneuver and offers less protection from the waves. Before you begin, consider which materials are suited to this building project.

Handmade Raft

A raft can be built out of any materials that float. Wood floats because it is less dense than water. A raft could also be pieced together from the garbage washed up on the beach. Hunt for items that are waterproof and hollow (and can be sealed so they do not fill with water). Options you might find include empty oil drums, plastic bottles, Styrofoam blocks, and aluminum cans. Any raft should be **symmetrical** to ensure that it is as stable as possible.

For propulsion, a raft needs a sail or a paddle. The wide surface of a fabric sail catches the wind. A paddle may be single-bladed (with a flat sheet to push against the water at only one end) or double-bladed. The wider the blade of a paddle, the more powerful it will be, but the harder it will be to pull through the water.

Bamboo will make an excellent raft because its stems are hollow.

Make a Raft
From your list of supplies and local materials, you will need to make:

→ A raft that will float on water
→ A paddle for propulsion.

Can You Make It?

Step 1
Think about which local materials would be best suited to making your raft. Use your ax if necessary.

Step 2
Which item in your backpack could tie your raft together?

Step 3
Which item in your backpack could be used for propulsion?

Step 4
Could you make any modifications to your raft or paddle using local materials or items washed up on the beach?

Raft

Secure fastening

CHAPTER 6
GET HELP

If you decide to stay on land and wait for rescue, you will improve your chances of survival by sending a distress signal. There are many ways you can enlist your maker skills to help with this important task.

Smoke
Alexander Selkirk was rescued when he ran along the beach waving a flaming branch (see page 10–11). Since you know how to light a fire using your mirror, you can use the same strategy. Three fires arranged in a triangle is an internationally recognized distress signal. If you light fires on the beach, they will be seen from the horizon, which is around 3 miles (5 km) away. If you light them on higher, open ground, they will be seen from farther away. For example, if your island has a hill 300 feet (91 m) high, fires on its peak could be seen for around 20 miles (32 km).

At night, your flames will be clear in the darkness. During the day, turn your smoke from grayish white to dark gray by burning damp leaves. Burning rubber items washed up on the beach will create thick, black smoke. If you try this, do not breathe in the fumes.

This beach fire can be seen for around 3 miles (5 km) out to sea.

Mirror, Mirror

Your mirror can perform another vital task if you spot a ship passing on the horizon or see a plane flying overhead. Use the mirror to reflect the sun's rays into the eyes of the captain or lookout. Flash this signal on and off, so that your rescuer recognizes that a human is deliberately making a signal. If the ship or plane comes closer to take a look at you, hold your arms overhead to form a Y shape. This is an international distress signal.

FIERCE FACT!
During World War II, John F. Kennedy and his crew mates were marooned for six days on Olasana, in the Pacific, after their **torpedo boat** sank.

Making a Y with your arms and body means: "Yes, I do need help."

MESSAGE IN A BOTTLE

In some movies, a person marooned on a desert island would seal a message in a bottle and throw it out to sea. In real life, could sending a message in a bottle really get you rescued?

Drifting Bottles

In the past, scientists hoping to learn more about ocean currents would often release bottles into the ocean. They released thousands of "drift bottles" and studied where they ended up, sometimes decades later. In the twenty-first century, scientists have replaced drift bottles, which harm ocean life and habitats, with drift cards that biodegrade, or decay, as they float.

A Tiny Chance

Studies of drift bottles show that only about 3 percent of released bottles are recovered. Most bottles sink within a few months from the weight of the tiny ocean creatures that attach themselves. However, there are stories of messages in bottles being found decades later. In 2014, a German fisherman found a bottle containing a postcard written in 1913. It had been thrown off the German coast as an experiment by a man named Richard Platz. The postcard was given to Platz's granddaughter, since he had died in 1946.

There are very few examples of people being rescued as a result of a message in a bottle. One rescue did take place in 2005, when 88 South American **migrants** were stranded aboard a broken-down boat. When they saw the long nets of a fishing boat floating by, they tied a bottle to them with an **SOS**. When the bottle was hauled in, they were rescued. Given the small chance of a free-floating bottle being discovered, it would be safest not to rely on them for rescue. If you do, be prepared for a long wait.

POST CARD.

One Shilling Reward.
Eine Mark Belohnung.
Twaalf Stuivers Belooning.

Card No.. 57

Please fill up blanks on back of this Card and put in the Post.

Bitte die nötigen Einträge an der Rückseite zu machen, und die Karte der Post zu übergeben.

Wees zoo goed deze kaart intevullen en aan de post overgeven.

No Stamp Required.

Keine Marke erforderlich.

Geen Mark noodig.

G. P. BIDDER,
C/O
**The Marine Biological
Association,
PLYMOUTH,
ENGLAND.**

This postcard was launched in a drift bottle in 1906. It was found in 2015.

A message in a bottle probably offers a less than 1 percent chance of rescue.

FIERCE FACT!
Messages attached to balloons were released from the French city of Paris when the Prussian army surrounded it in 1870–1871.

WRITE LARGE

Another way to send a distress signal is to "write" in big letters on the beach, using bright-colored clothing or logs. The international distress signal is "SOS," or you could just write "HELP."

You Survived!

Using your ax, you cut several large branches and use them to form the letters SOS on the wide beach. Your letters are 15 feet (5 m) high, so they can be seen from the air. To make your signal even move visible, you decorate the letters with shiny metal items that have washed up on the shore. Just when you have given up hope, you hear a plane flying overhead. You run onto the beach, holding your arms to form a Y. The plane turns and dips, heading back toward the island. You will soon be on your way home.

Your ordeal is over! You wave goodbye to your desert island as you fly toward the nearest inhabited land.

ANSWERS—
DID YOU MAKE IT?

Did your makerspace survival skills pass the test? Did you select the best equipment for each "Make It Out Alive'" activity? Check your choices against the answers below.

Page 19 Fish Trap

Large plastic bottle • Craft knife
To make the trap, you will need a large plastic bottle and a craft knife. Take the bottle cap off. Cut the top off the bottle about one-third of the way down. Turn this section around, and press it inside the base of the bottle. Put sand or stones inside to weigh it down.

Page 29 Raised Bed

2 broom handles • Duct tape
Craft knife
To build the frame, wrap the duct tape around and between the broom handles to make the net. Make strong supports from duct tape, both at right angles and diagonally to the broom handles. Flat stones could be used to build two platforms.

Page 33 Mosquito Net

20 metal bottle caps • Thread
Nylon netting, 13 x 9 feet (4 x 3 m)
Sewing needle • Pair of scissors
Strong cord, 7 feet (2 m) long
Use the nylon net as your mosquito net. Using the needle and thread, stitch a hem around the edges, into which you can place the bottle caps to use as small weights. If you cannot sew, use duct tape. Look for sticks about 3 feet (1 m) long to use as posts. Tie the cord between them. Drape the net over the posts and cord, with its longest sides running head-to-toe above the bed.

Page 39 Raft

Coil of rope • Table tennis racket
To build the raft, find six logs and six thinner branches. Lay the logs side by side. Lay the branches in pairs at right angles to the logs, with three on top and three beneath. Tie securely with rope, around and between every log. Use the table tennis racket to propel your raft forward. You could modify your raft by using oil drums, Styrofoam, or other recycled materials to add buoyancy.

GLOSSARY

aquifer A layer of rock that holds groundwater.

buoyant Able to float.

castaway A person who is stranded in a place where there are no other people, usually because of a shipwreck.

colonized Moved into by a new species of plant or animal.

condenses Changes from a gas into a liquid.

continent One of the world's seven main expanses of land: Africa, Antarctica, Asia, Australasia, Europe, North America, and South America.

coral reef Mound or ridge formed of living coral and coral skeletons.

currents Continuous movements of water in one direction.

dehydrated Suffering from extreme loss of water from the body; symptoms include thirst, headaches, confusion, and eventually death.

dense Closely packed.

distilling Separating a liquid mixture using evaporation and condensation.

evaporates Turns from a liquid into a vapor or gas.

fiber Thin thread of animal, plant, or man-made material.

groundwater Water held underground in the soil or in holes in rock.

hardiest Most able to survive in difficult conditions.

hull The bottom and sides of a boat.

malaria A disease caused by a parasite that is spread by mosquitoes.

mammals Animals that give birth to live young and feed them with milk.

marooned Trapped and alone on an island or other remote place.

migrants People who travel to another place looking for a safer or better life.

musket An old gun with a long barrel.

native A kind of plant or animal that originally grew or lived in a particular place.

nutritious Containing substances that a person needs to be healthy.

outrigger canoes Narrow boats with one or more floats attached to the sides.

sea level The average height of the ocean's surface.

SOS An internationally recognized distress signal.

species A group of similar living things that can breed with each other.

still A device that uses evaporation and condensation for separating liquid mixtures.

streamlined Describes something with a sleek shape that can move swiftly through water or air.

submerged Covered by water.

symmetrical Having sides or halves that are the same.

tides The rising and falling of the ocean, usually twice each day, caused by the pull of the moon and sun.

torpedo boat A small warship armed with underwater missiles.

tropical In an area around the equator, where it is hot and often rainy.

uninhabited Not lived in by people.

venomous Able to inject a poisonous substance.

Zika virus A disease usually spread by particular species of mosquitoes.

FURTHER READING

Books

Kogan Ray, Deborah. *The Impossible Voyage of Kon-Tiki*. Watertown, MA: Charlesbridge, 2015.

Levete, Sarah. *Maker Projects for Kids Who Love Woodworking* (Be a Maker!). St. Catharines, ON: Crabtree Publishing, 2016.

Long, Denise. *Survivor Kid: A Practical Guide to Wilderness Survival*. Chicago, IL: Chicago Review Press, 2011.

O'Shei, Tim. *How to Survive on a Deserted Island* (Prepare to Survive). North Mankato, MN: Capstone Press, 2009.

Websites

Due to the changing nature of Internet links, PowerKids Press has developed an online list of websites related to the subject of this book. This site is updated regularly. Please use this link to access the list: www.powerkidslinks.com/ms/desertisland

INDEX